STE
Science
Technology
Engineering
Arts
&
Mathematics
GLOBAL
WARMING
Sheryl Recinos

Water Bear Press

Paperback: 978-1-951542-44-3
Ebook: 978-1-951542-45-0

Los Angeles, California

Our climate is changing.
This is called global warming.

Global warming is happening because humans create too much waste, and this leads to big changes in the weather.

We use too many
greenhouse gases.

Greenhouse gases include carbon dioxide and methane gas.

Carbon dioxide is released through chemical reactions. It is also released when animals breathe.

Methane is produced from livestock, or farm animals. It mainly is released from pigs, chickens, and cattle.

Fossil fuels are used for energy, but we are using them faster than they can be made.

Coal, oil, and natural gas
are fossil fuels.

When there are too many greenhouse gases in the air, this increases the temperature across the planet.

As our temperatures increase, there are more wildfires and heat waves.

Glaciers in the Arctic have
begun to melt.

As ice melts into the ocean,
the temperature level of the
ocean increases.

Warmer ocean water causes more liquid water to evaporate into water vapor, which is the gas form of water.

The increase of water vapor in the air adds to the greenhouse gases.

The weather begins to change, resulting in a shift in climate across the globe.

Storms become more intense.

Extreme weather becomes more common.

Hurricanes are scarier and deadlier.

Snow falls in places that are not prepared for snow.

As our world's climate changes, people and animals are in danger.

Places that used to grow enough food face droughts.

Other places can have massive floods from unexpected rainfall.

Infections can spread more easily.

The world is changing because of global warming.

If we don't do something soon, we will cause irreversible damage to the environment.

This means that we cannot fix it in our lifetime.

What can we do to help reduce global warming?

We need to reduce the amount of fossil fuels that we use.

Some schools have a special day of the week when everyone walks instead of driving.

We can buy foods that are grown locally, so that the drivers don't have to use too much gas to transport them.

We can reuse bags when we go to the store.

We can be careful about using only what we need.

Everyone has a part to do in the fight against global warming.

What ideas do you have?

Glossary:

Carbon dioxide: a gas that has no color or odor and is made by burning carbon-based compounds and by cellular respiration in animals (when animals exhale or breathe out)

Climate: the weather conditions in an area over a long period of time

Evaporate: when a liquid of a substance changes into the gas form of the same substance

Global warming: a slow increase in Earth's temperature over time, which is caused by increased amounts of greenhouse gases in the atmosphere

Greenhouse gases: a gas that is dangerous for the environment in increased amounts, such as carbon dioxide or methane gas

Glossary:

Irreversible: unable to be reversed or changed

Methane gas: a gas that has no color or odor and is released as a waste product from livestock, released from tiny organisms that live at the bottom of the ocean, and can be made in factories

Water vapor: the gas form of water

Resources:

American Museum of Natural History
https://www.amnh.org/explore/ology/climate-change

NASA Climate Change for Kids
https://climatekids.nasa.gov/climate-change-meaning/

Time for Kids
https://www.timeforkids.com/g34/global-warming/

About the Author

Sheryl Recinos is an author and a physician. She enjoys science and writes children's books about science and medical history.

When she isn't writing, she is hanging out with her husband, kids, and all their pets. Her family has a "zoo" of animals: dogs, cats, turtles, tortoises, a tarantula, fish, and even a snake!

Her website is at: sherylrecinosmd.com

Printed in Great Britain
by Amazon

59304521R00031